Cool Papa Bell

Lightning-Fast Center Fielder

STARS
OF THE
NEGRO
LEAGUES

Cool Papa Bell

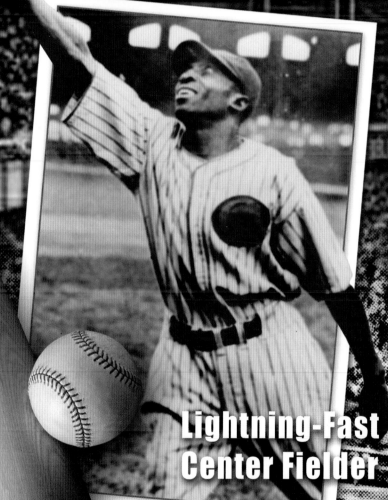

Lightning-Fast Center Fielder

E **Enslow Publishing**
101 W. 23rd Street
Suite 240
New York, NY 10011
USA
enslow.com

Hallie Murray

Published in 2020 by Enslow Publishing, LLC.
101 W. 23rd Street, Suite 240, New York, NY 10011

Cataloging-in-Publication Data

Names: Murray, Hallie.
Title: Cool Papa Bell: lightning-fast center fielder / Hallie Murray.
Description: New York : Enslow Publishing, 2020. | Series: Stars of the negro leagues | Includes bibliographic references and index. | Audience: Grades 7–12.
Identifiers: ISBN 9781978510500 (library bound) | ISBN 9781978510494 (pbk.)
Subjects: LCSH: Bell, Cool Papa, 1903–1991—Juvenile literature. | Baseball players—United States—Biography—Juvenile literature. | African American baseball players—United States—Biography—Juvenile literature. | Negro leagues—History—Juvenile literature.
Classification: LCC GV865.B343 M87 2020 | DDC 796.357092 [B]—dc23

Printed in the China

To Our Readers: We have done our best to make sure all website addresses in this book were active and appropriate when we went to press. However, the author and the publisher have no control over and assume no liability for the material available on those websites or on any websites they may link to. Any comments or suggestions can be sent by email to customerservice@enslow.com.

Portions of this book originally appeared in *Cool Papa Bell* by Shaun McCormack.

Photo Credits: Cover, p. 3 (inset photo Cool Papa Bell), pp. 18–19, 33, 39, 62–63, 74–75 National Baseball Hall of Fame and Museum; cover, pp. 3, 7, 11, 27, 43, 60, 76 (background), pp. 16–17 Library of Congress Prints and Photographs Division; cover, p. 3 (bat and ball) Mike Flippo/Shutterstock.com; pp. 9, 24, 34–35 The Sporting News/Getty Images; pp. 12–13 Buyenlarge/Archive Photos/Getty Images; pp. 22, 30–31 Diamond Images/Getty Images; pp. 40–41, 49, 85, 87 Bettmann/Getty Images; pp. 46–47 Ron Vesely/Getty Images; p. 52 Pictorial Parade/Archive Photos/Getty Images; pp. 54–55 George Silk/The LIFE Picture Collection/Getty Images; pp. 58, 68–69, 81 Transcendental Graphics/Getty Images; p. 65 Allan Grant/The LIFE Picture Collection/Getty Images; p. 71 Library of Congress/Corbis Historical/Getty Images; p. 78 Dilip Vishwanat/Getty Images; cover, pp. 1, 3 (baseball graphic) Kano07/Shutterstock.com; interior pages (glove) Sergiy1975/Shutterstock.com; interior pages (diamond graphic) Viktorija Reuta/Shutterstock.com.

Contents

Introduction

When people think about the fastest player in baseball, who comes to mind? Today, you might think of Billy Hamilton. Someone who watched baseball in the 1980s and '90s might say Rickey Henderson. Maybe someone even older would bring up Mickey Mantle. Very few people, if any, would mention Cool Papa Bell, though he was said to be one of the fastest players of the early twentieth century, maybe even all of baseball history, though there is no way to know for sure.

Cool Papa Bell was an amazingly fast center fielder who played baseball professionally from 1922 to 1942. Many people haven't heard of him because he never had the chance to play in the major leagues. In fact, no black players were allowed to play in the major leagues until 1947, when Jackie Robinson made his debut playing for the Brooklyn Dodgers. For most of the first half of the twentieth century, baseball, just like the rest of American society at that time, was segregated.

Black and white players weren't legally allowed to play on the same teams.

Because they weren't allowed to join major league teams, black baseball players formed their own teams and leagues. They worked together with businessmen and black communities and organized the Negro Leagues. This gave black ballplayers an opportunity to play organized baseball. Talented players surfaced in the leagues, and fans came to watch them showcase their talent. Together, the leagues they created were known as the Negro Leagues.

The Negro Leagues grew, strengthened, and emerged from the shadows during the 1930s and 1940s. The Negro Leagues are an important part of American history. The best African American ball clubs, like the Pittsburgh Crawfords and Homestead Grays, were led by legends like James "Cool Papa" Bell, Satchel Paige, Josh Gibson, and others. These clubs were able to rise above the major league teams they were barred from playing against in end-of-the-year, barnstorming rivalries. Time after time, in thousands of hard-fought games, the players of the Negro Leagues proved themselves equal to or better than the big league players and revealed what American baseball fans were losing as a result of segregation in baseball.

Many Negro League players were equal to major league players. Many were even better, but their achievements have gone largely unrecognized because of racism. In 1971, Satchel Paige became the first Negro League player inducted into the Baseball Hall of Fame. Baseball historians and fans had started to realize that it was important to appreciate and memorialize the talents of players who were barred from participating from the majors despite their skills and

Cool Papa Bell in a Pittsburgh Crawfords uniform circa 1934. Bell was said to be the fastest man in the Negro Leagues and was among the fastest players in all of baseball history.

talents. Over the next thirty-five years, thirty more Negro League players were inducted into the Baseball Hall of Fame, including Cool Papa Bell, who became a member in 1974. It doesn't fix the unfairness of segregation, but by learning about these players, we can at least honor their achievements and remember them as the legends they were.

Chapter 1

Baseball Under jim Crow

Long before he was known as "Cool Papa," James Thomas Bell was born on May 17, 1903, near a small farming town called Starkville, Mississippi. Starkville was a small farming town, and Bell's father, Jonas, was a sharecropper who farmed cotton and corn. His mother, Mary Nichols was part Native American. Like Bell's father, she also farmed and sometimes performed odd jobs around the community. Bell had little interest in farming, though. He only wanted to play baseball!

The Bell family was not wealthy, though, with two parents, four daughters, and three sons, so the kids had to work as well. Instead of farming, Bell worked at the Agricultural and Mechanical College in Starkville (now Mississippi State University) in the creamery and the agricultural experiment station. When he was seventeen, he left Starkville and moved to St. Louis, Missouri, which is where his baseball career really began.

Bell's father was a sharecropper, a farmer who farmed another person's land and then paid a portion of their crops as rent. In this photo, a cotton farmer cultivates his crop in 1902.

Bell's birth in 1903 occurred less than fifty years after the end of the Civil War, when African American slaves were freed by the Emancipation Proclamation and the Thirteenth Amendment. But freedom was just the first step, and African Americans still lived with legally enforced discrimination and racism. White politicians, especially in the south, created laws that limited African Americans' civil rights and financial opportunities. These laws were known as Jim Crow laws. In many ways, the Negro Leagues were created as a direct response to Jim Crow laws and the segregation they enforced.

Jim Crow Laws

The years following the end of the Civil War are known to historians as the "Reconstruction Era." During this time, federal laws were created to help African Americans gain more rights, including the Fourteenth Amendment, which defined who was a citizen of the United States and forbid states from limiting the rights of such citizens, and the Fifteenth Amendment, which gave all citizens the right to vote regardless of race. But during the 1870s, white supremacist politicians began to regain power, especially in the South, and by 1877 these politicians had gained control of every southern state, marking the end of the Reconstruction Era.

In the following years, new laws were created that called for segregated schools, bathrooms, libraries, and other public facilities. These laws were called "Jim Crow laws" after a popular racist song-and-dance act performed by a white person in blackface. Although slavery was now illegal, white America's acceptance of blacks as equals was slow in coming. Jim Crow laws restored the inferior status of African Americans after the Civil War ended in 1865.

Jim Crow laws were the written code that blocked emancipated slaves from the rights and privileges given to white people. Black and white Americans could not sit together on buses, on trains, or in restaurants. They were forbidden from drinking from the same water fountains. These laws used the term "separate but equal" to justify segregation, because it was legal to require that black and white people use different facilities as long as they were equal in quality. In reality, however, the segregated public facilities provided for African Americans were usually in much worse condition than the white facilities. The term "separate and unequal" would have been more appropriate.

Sports were no exception. Even though baseball had been integrated when Americans first started playing in the 1860s, black players found themselves shut out of

Plessy v. Ferguson

The term "separate but equal" comes from a 1896 Supreme Court case called *Plessy v. Ferguson* brought by a man named Homer Plessy who was kicked out of a "whites only" train car because he was one-eighth African American. Plessy's lawyers argued that removing Plessy from the railroad car was a violation of his thirteenth and fourteenth amendment rights. Unfortunately, the court disagreed and ruled that institutions could have separate facilities for people of different races as long as the facilities were equal. The concept of "separate but equal" paved the way for laws enforcing segregation and other Jim Crow laws. It took a long time to reverse the effects of *Plessy v. Ferguson*, but cases like *Brown v. Board of Education* (1954) have since made segregation illegal.

This political cartoon implies that Jim Crow laws and race will affect even new technology, like airships.

more and more clubs as the nineteenth century went on. By 1900, Jim Crow laws had cast a shadow over the game of baseball.

Baseball Officially Becomes Segregated

In the late 1800s and early 1900s, Georgia passed legislation that read, "It shall be unlawful for any amateur white baseball team to play baseball on any vacant lot or baseball diamond within two blocks of a playground devoted to the Negro race, and it shall be unlawful for any amateur colored baseball team to play baseball in any vacant lot or baseball diamond within two blocks of any playground devoted to the white race." This meant not only that blacks and whites couldn't play together but also that they couldn't even play anywhere near each other.

As early as 1867, the nominating committee of the National Association of Baseball Players drew baseball's color line. The committee unanimously came out against "the admission of any club which may be composed of one or more colored persons." The NABBP eventually disbanded, but its successor, the National Association of Professional

The Cuban Giants, pictured here circa 1885, were one of the first professional baseball teams formed entirely of African American players.

Base Ball Players, upheld baseball's racist philosophy with an unwritten rule that barred African Americans from its teams and leagues. This racist exclusion is what brought the Negro Leagues into existence.

By 1900, there were five all-black professional teams: the Cuban Giants, whose home city varied from year to year; the New York Cuban X Giants; the Norfolk, Virginia, Red Stockings; the Chicago Unions; and the Chicago Colombian Giants. African American teams flourished in the North and Midwest. By 1906, nine African American teams had appeared within 100 miles of Philadelphia.

In 1910, the first effort was made to establish a Negro League that included teams from all over the country—from Chicago, Louisville, New Orleans, St. Louis, Kansas City, and Columbus. African American baseball leaders said they would pay up to $300 each for a franchise in the league. Unfortunately, the league dwindled before the league played its first game, and it would take another ten years before the first strong Negro League was established.

The Start of the Negro Leagues

Tens of thousands of former slaves picked up their belongings and headed north every year in the early 1900s. By 1916, there were professional African American teams in almost every large city in the North and West. The Duval Giants of Jacksonville, Florida, also made the trip in 1916. Because there was little opportunity for an all-black ball club in the South at that time, the entire team picked up and headed north. They changed their name to the Bacharach Giants and settled in Atlantic City, New Jersey.

In 1920, the first viable Negro League—the Negro National League—was born. It began with eight teams: the Chicago American Giants, the Indianapolis ABCs, the Chicago Giants, the Kansas City Monarchs, the St. Louis Giants, the Detroit Stars, the Dayton Marcos, and the Cuban Stars. Owners of each team paid $500 to join the league. Many teams took the name of the Giants because by then major league baseball's New York Giants had become very successful. Many African American teams used "Cuban" or "Colombian" in their names to avoid discrimination. They believed Americans would be more tolerant of Central American players than African American players.

Andrew "Rube" Foster, the manager of the Chicago American Giants, is given credit for starting the Negro National League. His efforts earned him a spot in the National Baseball Hall of Fame. Foster suggested that the Negro National League fashion itself after the major leagues. Part of his effort was dedicated to ensuring that players didn't betray their teams in the middle of a season. Many teams were damaged when their players quit. Foster sought to establish a more civilized game. This idea didn't always play out the way Foster wanted. Many players—especially Bell's teammate Satchel Paige—did skip games, break contracts, and ditch their teams when the owners of other teams offered them more money. But Foster's Negro National Field created some order out of the chaos and gave the more stable all-black teams a community of other franchises to compete against.

Andrew "Rube" Foster was a famous pitcher in the first decade of the twentieth century, but today he is better known as the founder of the first lasting league for professional black teams, the Negro National League, which he founded in 1920.

Bell's Big Break

The year the Negro National League was founded, 1920, was the year that seventeen-year-old James Bell left Starkville, Mississippi, to move to St. Louis, Missouri, to live with his brothers and attend high school. His plan was to work during the day and attend night school, but that plan didn't work out. Bell lived near a park, and instead of school Bell ended up playing baseball in the evenings.

Bell's brothers were also baseball players, and the three Bell boys played together on an all-black semipro team called the Compton Hill Cubs. Bell earned a name for himself with his keen hitting skills, blazing speed, and dazzling center field performance, but with the Compton Hill Cubs the five-foot-eleven, 145-pound Bell signed on as a knuckleball pitcher. With his knuckleball, Bell had a pitch to baffle batters. When throwing the pitch, he would wind up and release the baseball so that it left his hand without any rotation on it.

While hurling knuckleballs for the Compton Hill Cubs, Bell was earning a modest $21.20 per week laboring at the Independent Packing Company. He attended high school at night. In August of 1921, the Compton Hill Cubs disbanded. Bell then joined another semipro team, the East St. Louis Cubs, in 1922. With his new team, Bell earned $20 per week for his pitching performances on Sundays.

That spring, Bell got his first big break. He tried out and made the cut for the St. Louis Stars, a powerhouse in the Negro National League. With the Stars, Bell was able to earn $90 per month. In 1922, his first full season with the Stars, Bell batted over .400 in about 60 at-bats. He slugged

Bell played for the St. Louis Stars from 1922 to 1931. He was originally a pitcher for the Stars, but in 1924 he began to transition to playing more in the outfield, and today he is best remembered as a center fielder.

three doubles, a triple, and three home runs. While playing for the Stars, Bell hit well over .300 seven times. Records show he hit 15 home runs in 1926 and 11 of them in 1925.

The St. Louis Stars

Over the first twelve years of the Negro National League's existence, the Chicago American Giants were the strongest team. They were the only team that remained in the league for each of those years. The city of St. Louis was always represented in the league, but its club ownership changed hands. The St. Louis Giants franchise became the St. Louis Stars in 1921.

Scheduling games was always a problem because none of the teams could afford a home stadium. Many clubs signed deals to lease ball parks from white teams. Negro teams would play their home games when the white teams were on the road.

With these arrangements, it was almost impossible to create a schedule of games that would be fair to all clubs. Records show that it was rare for all teams to play the same number of games. In 1921, the Chicago American Giants won the championship for the second time. The Kansas City Monarchs, who came in second place that year, played 62 games. The last-place Chicago Giants were able to play only 42 games.

The St. Louis Stars improved almost immediately after Bell joined the team. In his first year, they won 23 and lost 23. By 1924, the team was much more competitive, winning 40 and losing 36. The Stars finished in second place in the first half of 1925 with a record of 31 and 14, trailing the mighty Kansas City Monarchs, who finished at

31 and 9. But in the second half of that season, the Stars played better than the Monarchs. They won 38 games and lost 12. Finally, in a playoff for the Negro National League pennant, the Monarchs edged Bell's Stars 4 games to 3.

The Stars had somewhat of a slump in 1926 and 1927, despite the excellent batting of Bell and his teammate Mule Suttles. In 1928, though, they rose to the top again and beat the Chicago American Giants 5 to 4 in the playoffs. They narrowly lost to the Monarchs again in 1929 but won the league in 1930. In 1931, the Negro National League disbanded, and so did the Stars, but because of their great record that season, they were awarded the pennant even though the season was never finished. After the Stars crumbled, Bell would go on to play for their frequent rivals for the pennant, the Kansas City Monarchs.

Chapter 2

Playing Professional Ball

In the early stages of his career, Bell was primarily a pitcher and made only sporadic appearances in the outfield. In 1924, at Stars manager Bill Gatewood's recommendation, Bell began working harder on his fielding skills. He began seeing more and more playing time in centerfield. Gatewood was responsible for two changes in Bell's play that would prove to be very important to his success: one was this move from pitcher to outfielder, while the other was in Bell's namc. Gatewood is the main reason Bell is known as "Cool Papa" today.

In his early days playing with the Stars, Bell went by his birth name, James. Bell was was known for his unbelievable speed, but his new nickname actually came from Bell's calm approach to stressful situations. In particular, it is said that he earned the nickname "Cool" after striking out Oscar Charleston, a well-known slugger who played for the Indianapolis ABCs. At six feet tall and nearly 200 pounds, Charleston was physically imposing, and he could run fast. He also had a reputation for picking fights. At bat, he was known for being a successful hitter with an excellent average: there were five seasons in which Charleston was said to have hit over .400, and his lifetime average was .357. One story says that Charleston once hit a ball so hard and so far over the fence that it made a pitcher cry.

Despite Charleston's fearsome reputation, Bell managed to strike him out with tricky knuckleballs. After this feat, players throughout the Negro Leagues started calling him "Cool," for keeping such a cool head in such a scary situation. But the Stars' manager, Bill Gatewood, felt like the name was incomplete. He added "Papa" to end of it, and the name "Cool Papa" stuck. Bell was known ever after as Cool Papa Bell, not James Thomas.

Into the Outfield

Despite his success with the knuckleball, Bell's real fame came from his skill at center field. Bell had always been a right-handed batter and a southpaw, meaning that he threw the baseball with his left hand, and left-handed pichers were in demand. But At Gatewood's suggestion, Bell scrapped his knuckleball and his pitching aspirations and began playing exclusively in center field. Next, he learned to bat from both sides of the plate. Bell eventually became a defensive specialist—an all-star and eventual Hall of Famer—in center field. Learning to switch hit also helped to give Bell a few extra steps on infielders. When he batted from the left side, he started out a few feet closer to

Southpaw

Because Bell was a southpaw, he was a valuable addition to any pitching rotation. The majority of major league pitchers are righthanded, but southpaws are proven to have a competitive edge against lefthanded batters, making left-handed pitchers a hot commodity in the major leagues. Some people believe the word "southpaw" comes from the fact that many early baseball diamonds were oriented so that the batter faced east. This meant the pitcher faced west, with his left arm on his south side. The most likely explanation, though, comes from another sport entirely: boxing. In boxing, a southpaw stance is one in which the fighter leads with their right, using their left arm to deliver the major punches. The association of the southpaw stance with left-handed athletes migrated over to baseball, where southpaw now means a left-handed pitcher.

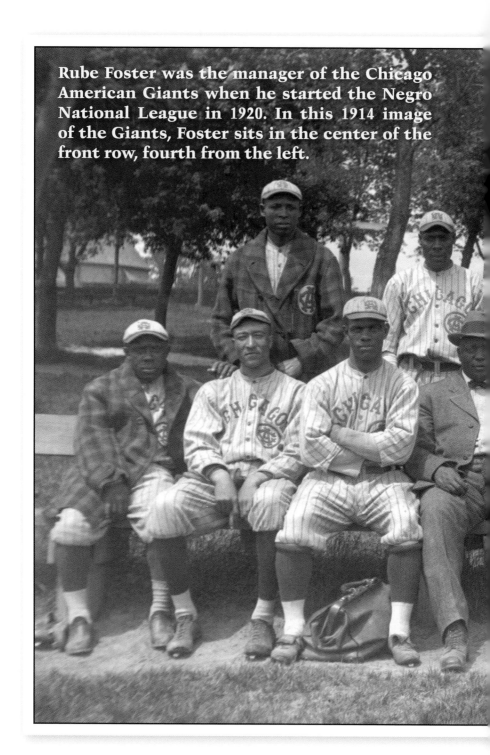

Rube Foster was the manager of the Chicago American Giants when he started the Negro National League in 1920. In this 1914 image of the Giants, Foster sits in the center of the front row, fourth from the left.

first base. It's impossible to tell just how much this helped him, but it could have played a part in Bell legging out hundreds of his base hits.

Bell did not have the strongest arm in the league. This was evident from his pitching style. He had always relied on finesse and accuracy instead of a blazing fastball to get hitters out. What his arm lacked, however, his legs more than made up for. Bell's speed was unmatched. He was known for playing extremely shallow in center field. He was able to charge in to catch balls hit just over the heads of shortstops and second basemen in front of him. Even though he played shallow, baseballs rarely sailed past him. Cool Papa was able to sprint deep into the outfield from shallow center to make catches that would have sailed past many outfielders who played much deeper than he did.

Bell's fame began to grow shortly after he became a center fielder. He was playing every day now, so people were seeing a lot more of him. His base-running feats brought him the reputation of being the fastest player in baseball. Bell said himself that he stole 175 bases in 200 games during the 1933 season. He was able to taunt and distract pitchers once he reached base. This made it easier for the hitters that batted behind him in the lineup. The pitcher would be so worried about Bell stealing bases that his concentration would be lost. Bell was the prototypical lead-off hitter. To this day, major league baseball teams look for lead-off hitters that display the same types of skills that Bell had.

Owners and managers look for fast runners with a "good eye." Having a good eye means that the hitter is a good judge of balls and strikes. Good lead-off hitters

Bell became known for his speed both rounding the bases and in the outfield, where his quick running helped him pick up balls and his early pitching experience helped him throw them far back into the infield.

usually have a high on-base percentage, which is the total number of walks and hits divided by the number of at-bats they have. They don't have to get base hits; they just have to get on base. A player with a high onbase percentage is valuable at the top of a lineup because he can get on base and set the stage for the sluggers in the middle of the lineup.

No one wanted to walk Bell because that would put him on first. He would usually he able to steal second and third base. If there was a base hit, Bell could usually score from first base. Allowing him to get on base was a tragedy for opposing pitchers since it usually meant that he would score.

It is said that Bell won the 1934 East-West All-Star Game by drawing a walk and stealing second base in the eighth inning. Bell reportedly scored the game's only run on a soft hit by Jud Wilson of the Philadelphia Stars. Bell breezed around the bases, scoring easily from second base to secure a 1-0 victory for starting pitcher Satchel

Paige and the East All-Stars. This happened again and again throughout his career. It is the main reason that he was such a dangerous player.

Bell played for the Homestead Grays in 1932 and from 1943 to 1946. Here, he can be seen rounding the bases in a Grays uniform in 1932.

Several years later, in 1948, at the age of forty-five, Bell rounded the bases and scored from first on a sacrifice bunt in an exhibition barnstorming game against the American League's Cleveland Indians. Even in the twilight of his career, Bell could run with the best of them. Bell ended up spending ten years with the St. Louis Stars. With Bell, shortstop Willie Wells—who was said to have been Bell's closest friend—and first baseman Mules Suttles, the Stars became a Negro National League powerhouse. The team contended for Negro National League championships in 1929 and 1930 against the mighty Kansas City Monarchs.

"Little Ball"

In the 1920s and 1930s, the art of "little ball," that is, advancing runners from base to base through base hits and bunting, rather than swinging for home runs, was losing importance in the major leagues. Babe Ruth had stormed onto the scene and gotten the league to focus on home runs. Why risk getting out by trying for extra bases when the next batter might blast one over the fence? This was the all or nothing way of thinking that prevailed in the big leagues at the time.

Home runs were a big part of the Negro Leagues as well, with sluggers like Josh Gibson bashing baseballs over fences at will—if the field he played on even had a fence. But in the Negro Leagues, little ball and baserunning still flourished. Drawing walks, stealing bases, bunting, sacrificing to move runners into scoring position, and hustling on every play still played big parts in Negro League baseball games. Speed was very important. And Cool Papa was the best at doing these things. "We played a different kind of baseball than the white teams," Bell said. "We played tricky baseball. We did things they didn't expect. We'd bunt and run in the first inning. Then when they would come in for a bunt we'd hit away. We always crossed them up. We'd run the bases hard and make the fielders throw too quick and make wild throws. We'd fake a steal home and rattle the pitcher in to a balk."

Cool Papa's Unbelievable Speed

There were times when Bell would dash all the way in from center field to second base to catch a pick-off throw from the pitcher. According to Buck Leonard, a first baseman who batted behind Josh Gibson in the Homestead Grays' lineup, "Cool Papa Bell was about the best, and he was over the hill when I came up." Bill Yancey, a gifted shortstop who worked as a talent scout for the New York Yankees after playing for fourteen years in the Negro Leagues, said:

I haven't seen anybody yet could run with Cool. When I was on the Lincoln Giants, we played in a little park in New York called the Catholic Protectory up in the Bronx. That was our regular home field. Judy Johnson had been telling me about this guy that came to Cuba every winter, and Judy told me, "if the guy hits the ball on two hops on the ground you won't be able to throw him out from shortstop." Now I could throw, and I said nobody can outrun a baseball. So the first time Cool Papa came to New York with the St. Louis Stars, he hit the ball into right field. Chino Smith was out there, and he could field a ball, and if you made a wide turn at first base he could throw you out trying to hustle back. I went out to get the throw, and when I looked up Cool Papa was slowing up going into third. And I said to myself, "That sonofagun didn't touch second."

Some of Bell's contemporaries said that he was not only fast but tricky, too. " You had to watch him on the bases," said Jack Marshall. "I saw him go from first to third and he never even touched second. He ran inside it by three feet when the umpire wasn't looking!"

But Yancey was still amazed by Bell's speed. "Next time up he hit another one about the same place. Now nobody got a three-base hit in that little park, I don't care where they hit the ball. And I watched this guy run. Well, he came across second base and it looked like his feet weren't touching the ground! And he never argued, never said anything. That was why they called him Cool Papa; he was a real gentleman."

Racism in the South

During Bell's prime, about a third of all major league players were from the South. They would not play with or against African Americans. African Americans could not travel with white major league clubs because many hotels would not accommodate them. Also, many baseball clubs held spring training in the South, where it was almost impossible for an African American to live peacefully. Organizations and hate groups like the Ku Klux Klan made life in the South miserable for African Americans.

The few African Americans who did play on white teams in white leagues before baseball's color line was officially drawn were often threatened. No matter how great their

Clarence "Fats" Jenkins and Bill Yancey of the New York Black Yankees, sometime in the mid-1930s. Yancey played professionally in the Negro Leagues from 1927 to 1936.

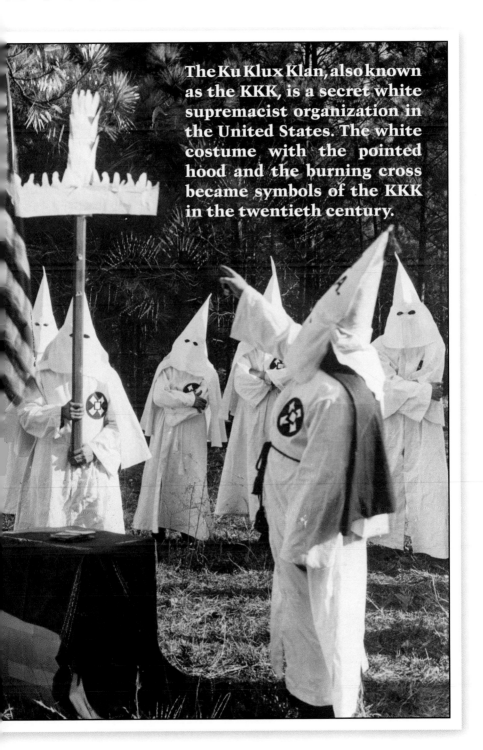

The Ku Klux Klan, also known as the KKK, is a secret white supremacist organization in the United States. The white costume with the pointed hood and the burning cross became symbols of the KKK in the twentieth century.

talent, owners and officials from Southern towns and cities would threaten teams that allowed African Americans to play with them. Racist Southerners, who refused to accept the fact that African Americans deserved the same rights that white men and women were given, feared losing to black teams.

Chapter 3

Legends of the Negro Leagues

Few, if any, Negro League teams played traditional schedules or kept accurate statistics, so the achievements of stars like Cool Papa Bell have survived mostly through storytelling and the memories of individual players. Legends have cropped up around Bell and his contemporaries, built out of stories from fans, reporters, and the players themselves, that seem almost unbelievable.

Some of the most amazing tales of the Negro Leagues are the ones about Cool Papa Bell's mind-blowing speed. It's said that once he stole two bases on a single pitch and that he was so fast he could run from first base to home on just a sacrifice bunt. The most famous legend about Bell is probably the time he stole 175 bases in a single 200-game season. This seems improbable based on modern statistics, but the game has changed so much since Cool Papa Bell's time that it could very well have happened. No one can say for sure whether it really did or not, but it's interesting to look at modern players and compare.

Few Negro Leagues players had the chance to really test themselves against Major League Baseball players, but if legends like that are even just partly true, players like Cool Papa Bell could definitely have held their own in the major leagues. The only thing stopping them was the segregation they faced from the organization and racism from club managers and owners. Bell's legendary 175-base season was in 1933. It would be fourteen more years before a black player joined the major leagues.

The Home Run Era

The standard for excellence in today's game is 50 stolen bases in a season. Few players do it. Since baseball ended its last players strike in 1994, baseballs have been flying over the fence like crazy. Little ball and speed are again losing importance. The last players to steal over 100 bases in a single 162-game season were center fielder Rickey Henderson of the American League and left fielder Vince Coleman of the National League, both of whom played in the 1980s. Henderson once stole 130 bases while playing with the Oakland Athletics in 1982. To steal 175 bases in one year is not impossible, but it is an amazing feat.

Since Henderson accomplished this feat in the mid 1980s, few players have gotten anywhere near it. Some players regularly steal more than fifty bases in a season, but they're rare. In the past fifteen years, only José Reyes has managed to steal over seventy bases in a season, with seventy-eight in 2007. In the 2018 season, the most bases

Too Good to Be True

Bell's feats of speed might seem improbably even modern statistics can be a little hard to believe. Both Mark McGwire and Barry Bonds have been accused of using performance-enhancing drugs, which might have helped them set their home run records. In 2013, because of scandals in the mid-2000s, Major League Baseball added random drug testing for performance-enhancing drugs throughout the season. The consequences for using these drugs have also been increased significantly. But players keep making new homerun records. In 2017, Aaron Judge broke the record for most homeruns by a rookie with fifty-two, surpassing previous record-holder McGwire, who hit forty-nine homeruns in 1987. Judge might go on to break other records too! Only time will tell.

Rickey Henderson played Major League Baseball from 1979 to 2003. He holds the MLB record for most bases stolen in a single season, with 130 from his 1982 season with the Oakland Athletics.

stolen by a single player was Whit Merrifield's forty-five, not even a third of Cool Papa Bell's storied 1933 season.

By contrast, since 1994, several players have hit more than 50 home runs in a single season. Mark McGwire in 1998 broke Roger Maris's thirty-eight-year single-season home run record by hitting 70 home runs. During that year, both he and Sammy Sosa had a season-long assault on Maris's record. Both of them surpassed this standard by the end of the season. The current record for home runs was set by Barry Bonds in 2001, with seventy-three home runs.

While not quite the "home run era" of the late 1990s and early 2000s, today's baseball still relies heavily on big hits to advance the game. There are many other possible reasons for the rise in homeruns outside of players' strength (real or artificial). Many baseball analysts say that the ball is "juiced," meaning that baseballs are manufactured differently so they can be hit farther. Others blame it on new baseball stadiums, which are much smaller than older ballparks. Because of expansion into new cities, the quality of pitching has declined. This has given sluggers the upper hand. They are able to prey on inexperienced or fading pitchers.

Fans love the drama associated with the home run, so it makes sense for owners to build their parks with shorter distances. The more home runs there are, the more fans there will be. More fans mean more ticket sales. This is the logic. If this trend continues, there may never again be another base stealer to come close to Bell's achievement of 175 stolen bases in a single season. Bell's accomplishment is hard to imagine, but some of the other tales associated with his game play stretch the imagination even further.

The Fastest Man in Baseball

Legend has it that when Bell was in his prime, he was the fastest man alive. Bell's friend and teammate, Satchel Paige, said that Olympic running champion Jesse Owens refused to race Bell because he knew he would lose. Bell routinely scored from first base on base hits and once scored from first on a bunt when he was forty-five years old. He often made it from first to third on infield ground outs.

One story, which was told time and time again by Satchel Paige, was that Bell was so fast that he could flick the light switch off and be in bed before the room was dark. Bell actually once rigged the light switch in his hotel room while Paige was out. Bell rigged it so that the lights would remain on for two or three seconds after the switch was turned off. When Paige came back and got in his bed, Bell flicked the switch and jumped into his own bed—before the lights went out!

Cool Papa Bell, left, stands in the dugout with Chicago American Giants manager Jim Taylor during a game in 1942. After the 1942 season, Bell finished out his career with four seasons with the Homestead Grays.

Infielders would yell frantically to each other and scramble in when Bell stepped to the plate. When he came up with two outs and no one on base, the infield would play extremely shallow, as if there was a runner at third with no outs. When there is a runner on third and fewer than two outs, coaches almost always bring the infield in so that the infielders have a chance to throw out the runner charging toward the plate. With the infield in, they are closer to home plate. The ball gets to them faster. But Bell forced managers to break convention. The infield would have to come in when he was up because they would not be able to throw him out at first if they played back. If Bell was on third with less than two outs, there was nothing that could stop him from scoring on a ground ball.

According to Jimmie Crutchfield, a teammate of Bell's on the Pittsburgh Crawfords, "[When] Bell hit one back to the pitcher, everybody would yell, 'Hurry!'" Teammate Judy John son said, " You couldn't play back in your regular position or you'd never throw him out." Bell was supposed to have been able to circle the bases in twelve seconds flat. The official major league record is 13.3 seconds. It was set by Evar Swanswon of the National League's Cincinnati Reds in 1931. Bell is also credited with hitting .437 in 1940 for Torreon of the Mexican league. In 89 games that year, Bell led the league with 119 runs, 167 hits, 15 triples, 12 home runs, and 79 runs batted in. Some records show that he hit .407 in 1944 and .402 in 1946. Other statistics show he hit as high as .409 in one year.

Many of Bell's achievements went unnoticed and unrecorded. "I remember one game I got five hits and stole five bases, but none of it was written down because they didn't bring the score book to the game that day," Bell said. It's impossible to tell how many bases he actually stole. One estimate says that he stole only 143 bases throughout his professional career. Other accounts say that he had more than that in almost every season he played.

Bill Veeck of the Cleveland Indians said this about Bell: "Defensively, he was the equal of Tris Speaker, Joe DiMaggio, or Willie Mays." Speaker, DiMaggio, and Mays were some of the greatest men to ever play baseball. Baseball scout Eddie Gottlieb said, "If he had played in the major leagues, he would have reminded fans of Willie Keeler as a hitter and Ty Cobb as a base runner-and he might have exceeded both." Both Keeler and Cobb dominated baseball's early years.

On the Field with Satchel Paige

Bell played on the Pittsburgh Crawfords for four years between 1933 and 1936 with legends Satchel Paige and Josh Gibson. With these superstars, the Crawfords won championships in 1933, 1935, and 1936.

Many say that Paige was the most talented pitcher to ever hurl a baseball. Bell certainly felt that he was one of the most dominating pitchers baseball has ever had. Paige was a showman as well, always wanting to entertain fans and make opponents look foolish. He had several names for his fastball, the "Bee Ball," the "Jump Ball," the "Trouble Ball," and the "Midnight Rider." Paige was able to throw his fastball over 90 miles per hour. While pitchers today regularly throw that fast, the thing that makes Satchel's fastball more impressive is that he threw it at

Bill Veeck had been a fan of Negro League players from a young age and had planned to bring these players into the majors even before he owned the Cleveland Indians. He brought Larry Doby onto the team in July 1947.

a time when there was less science and physical training used in baseball.

It wasn't until late in his career, when Paige was in his forties and fifties, that he developed a curveball. He had to because at that age, his arm had lost some of its juice. Most power pitchers—the New York Yankees' Roger Clemens is a perfect example—lose something off their fastball late in their careers. The best pitchers are able to compensate for this by developing other pitches. Paige was able to do this. By developing a number of off-speed pitches to keep hitters off-balance, Paige was able to finesse his way around batters and extend his incredibly long career.

Another pitch of Paige's, the "Windmill," confused batters and was banned when he finally did make it into the major leagues. Satchel would wind his arm up several times, spinning it around behind him. Before hurling it toward the plate, he would lean back, and pause for a moment before unleashing it. When he did release the ball, it was supposed to travel so fast that batters could not see it.

One Negro Leaguer, Biz Mackey, said that there were times when the ball Paige threw simply vanished into thin air. "A lot of pitchers have a fastball, but a very, very few—Feller, Grove, Johnson, a couple of others besides Satchel—have had that little extra juice that makes the difference between the good and the great man. When it's that fast, it will hop a little at the end of the line," Mackey said.

Mackey said this about Paige's best fastball as it approached the plate: "Beyond that, it tends to disappear. Yes, disappear. I've heard about Satchel throwing pitches that wasn't hit but that never showed up in the catcher's

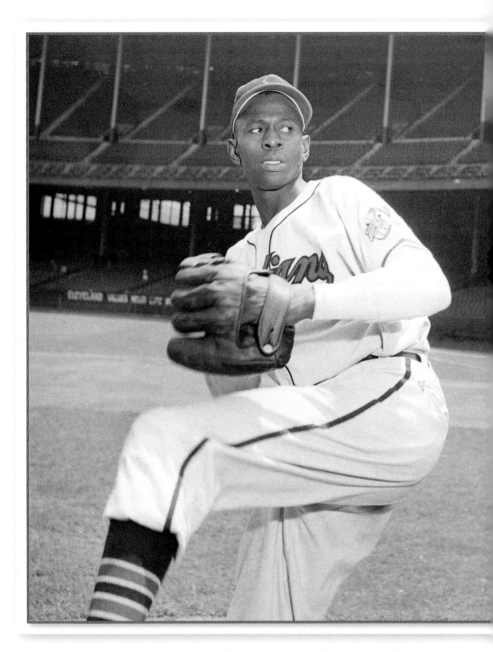

Satchel Paige is one of the most famous players to come out of the Negro Leagues. An amazing pitcher, Paige is remembered for his personality and charisma, as well as his great skill.

mitt nevertheless. They say the catcher, the umpire, and the bat boys looked all over for that ball, but it was gone. Now how do you account for that?"

Legendary Crawfords

On July 9, 1949, just after he turned forty-two years old, Paige again became a rookie. He became the first African American ever to pitch in the American League. He made a two-inning relief appearance for the Cleveland Indians in his major league debut. That year, he pitched in twenty-one games as a reliever, winning six and losing one. Paige is said to have pitched for African American barnstorming clubs through 1967, when he was sixty-one years old!

Records of his accomplishments after 1961 are scarce. By 1961, when his book *Maybe I'll Pitch Forever* came out, Paige estimated that he had pitched in more than 2,500 baseball games and won almost 2,000 of them. For three decades, between 1929 and 1958, he pitched almost every day. He played during the summers in

The Fastest Fastballs

As of 2018, the record for the fastest official fastball in the major leagues is tied between Aroldis Chapman of the New York Yankees and Jordan Hicks of the St. Louis Cardinals, at a blistering 105.1 miles per hour. Chapman made his MLB debut with the Cincinnati Reds in 2010 after playing in Cuba. He pitched for the Cubs in their winning 2016 World Series and reached 500 strikeouts faster than any pitcher in the history of the MLB. Hicks, on the other hand, made his MLB debut in 2018 at the age of twenty-one. With a pitch that moves over 100 miles per hour, like Chapman and Hicks', batters need to swing before the ball is even released to catch up with a ball that fast. This is what Mackey meant when he described Paige's fastball.

America and went down to the Dominican Republic, Cuba, or Mexico to spend his winters playing ball. Some days, he played two or three games. Paige claims he once pitched 153 games in a single year.

Throughout his career, Paige pitched for about 250 teams. He barnstormed for many different teams one game at a time to earn extra money. Before getting his first shot in the majors, Paige had pitched for the Pittsburgh Crawfords and Kansas City Monarchs, two of the Negro National League's most powerful ball clubs. Of all Negro League players, Satchel Paige was the best paid. It was probably a combination of his incredible talent and his willingness to entertain crowds.

Men who played with Paige say he often told sportswriters that he was going to strike out the first six or nine men he faced in a game. Many times, he kept his word. In other games, when his team was well ahead and had control of the game, he would call his outfield in, tell them to sit down, and proceed to strike out the next batter. This flair for the dramatic is what helped Paige earn up to $40,000 per year when he played with the Monarchs.

The accomplishments of Bell's Pittsburgh Crawfords teammate Josh Gibson also blurred the line between truth and legend. There is little doubt that Gibson was one of the mightiest sluggers ever to grace the baseball diamond. Many say he could hit more home runs—and longer ones— than legendary sluggers Babe Ruth, Hank Aaron, or Mark McGwire. Many record books show that Gibson hit 962 home runs over the course of his career. That is 200 more than Hank Aaron's official major league record.

Josh Gibson played in the Negro Leagues from 1930 to 1946, mostly for the Homestead Grays. Gibson was a major power hitter who was known for hitting unbelievable home runs.

It is also said that Gibson once hit 75 home runs in a single season, which is two more than the major league record, which Barry Bonds established in 2001. Gibson is supposed to have hit a ball completely out of Yankee Stadium. If this is true, it is the longest ball ever hit in the "House That Ruth Built," which is the stadium's nickname. Gibson's lifetime batting average was estimated to be .354.

Chapter 4

Dealing with Discrimination

Bell remained an extremely popular player over the course of his twenty-four-year career. In total, Bell played for seven professional teams: the St. Louis Stars, the Homestead Grays, the Detroit Wolves, the Kansas City Monarchs, the Pittsburgh Crawfords, the Memphis Red Sox, and the Chicago American Giants. He would go on to play for the Detroit Senators after retiring from professional ball.

One of the clearest measures of player popularity in the Negro Leagues was whether or not they were chosen to compete in the East-West All-Star Game. Fans got to choose the lineups for each team by voting for their favorite players in the newspaper. Due to his immense popularity, Bell was chosen to participate in the East-West All Star Game every year from its inception in 1933 through 1944, except for the years when he was playing in Latin America.

Teammates and fans alike marveled at Bell's speed, but they also admired his other skills, like the accuracy of his throws and his excellent batting average. His exceptional batting skills produced a .391 batting average in barnstorming exhibition games against major leaguers. The lowest estimate of his lifetime batting average is .341. In 1945, when he was past his prime and forty years old, Bell still ranked among the league leaders in stolen bases.

Other batting average estimates are higher. Some say his lifetime batting average was as high as .391 and that he batted over .400 several times in his career. He was not graced with the slugging power of contemporaries like Josh Gibson or Oscar Charleston, but what he lacked in power he made up for in speed. Bell was able to accumulate a high total of doubles and triples each year because of his quickness.

Breaking the Major League Color Line

Besides making a name for himself, Bell played a part in helping Jackie Robinson enter the major leagues. Robinson crossed Major League Baseball's color line in 1946. Brooklyn Dodgers' owner Branch Rickey felt that Robinson would be able to tolerate the racism and pressure he would be subjected to in the major leagues. Robinson was subjected to threats and ridicule throughout his career. In his first season, the pressure forced him into a slump, but he did recover and ended up having an impressive career that earned him a spot in the Baseball Hall of Fame in Cooperstown, New York.

When Robinson finally did make it to the Brooklyn Dodgers on opening day in 1947, he became the first African American to do so in over fifty years. It was not

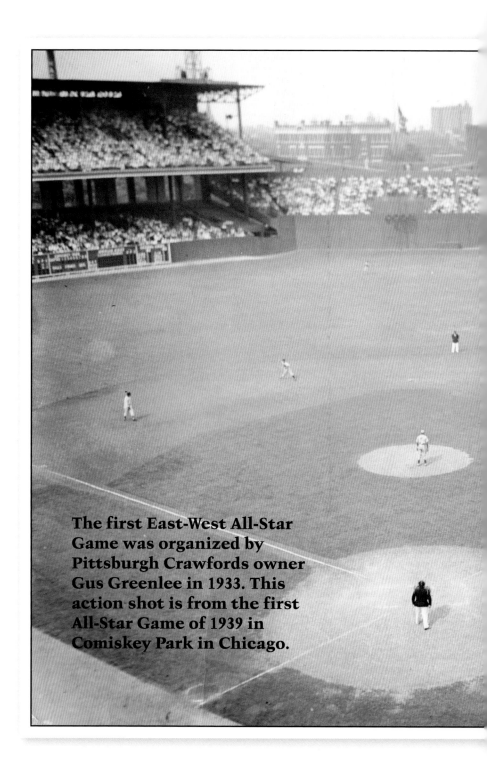

The first East-West All-Star Game was organized by Pittsburgh Crawfords owner Gus Greenlee in 1933. This action shot is from the first All-Star Game of 1939 in Comiskey Park in Chicago.

Batting Averages Today

When compared to major leaguers, there is little doubt that Bell could have been one of the best at any level of competition. Hitting .400 is a phenomenal achievement. Ted Williams was the last player to hit over .400 in a season. He hit .406 in 1941. The Hall of Fame slugger George Brett, who played for the American League's Kansas City Royals, hit .390 in 1980. Many people said that Tony Gwynn of the San Diego Padres, or Wade Boggs when he was in his prime playing for the Boston Red Sox, had the best chance of hitting .400, but neither of them ever did it. In the past five years, the highest batting average achieved by a MLB player is .348, which DJ LeMahieu managed in 2016 while playing for the Colorado Rockies. The last person to hit over .350 was Josh Hamilton, who hit .359 in 2010.

Jackie Robinson was the first black player in Major League Baseball since the league was first segregated in the nineteenth century. He played for the Brooklyn Dodgers from 1947 to 1956.

only a monumental day for Robinson, it was a monumental day for Bell, too. African Americans had finally been given a chance to prove that they could hit, catch, and run with anyone in the major leagues.

Bell took time to do whatever he could to help Robinson and other African American players make it into the major leagues. Robinson and Bell played together for a short period on the Kansas City Monarchs. When Robinson finally got the opportunity to start that fateful spring day in 1947, Bell said it was the greatest day of his life.

While scouts were eyeing Robinson and considering him for the major leagues in 1946, Bell was competing with Monte Irvin for the Negro National League batting title. Bell felt that he was too old to make the transition at that time. Major league club owners still wanted Negro League players to go through the minor leagues, and Bell felt that he just didn't have enough time to go through that. So in 1946, he threw the batting title so Irvin could take it. Scouts noticed how Irvin won the batting title that year, and it helped him to be picked to play for the New York Giants.

Moses Fleetwood Walker

While it is widely believed that Robinson was the first black man to play in the major leagues, this is not true. Robinson was the first black player in the major leagues after baseball was segregated in the late 1800s, but Moses Fleetwood Walker was the first African American major leaguer historically. Walker began playing professional ball in 1883 for Toledo, Ohio. When Toledo left the Northwestern League to enter the American Association the following year,

Walker went with the team and at that point became the first African American to play in the major leagues.

Fans' reactions to Walker were mixed. He was well received in the North, where sportswriters saluted him for making valuable contributions to the Toledo team. But in the South, things were different. In September of 1884, shortly before Toledo headed to Richmond, Virginia, for a three-game series, Toledo manager Charlie Morton received a letter from Richmond:

> We the undersigned do hereby warn you not to put up Walker, the Negro catcher, the evenings that you play in Richmond, as we could mention the names of 75 determined men who have sworn to mob Walker if he comes on the ground in a suit. We hope you will listen to our words of warning, so that there will be no trouble; but if you do not there certainly will be. We only write this to prevent much blood-shed, as you alone can prevent.

Walker had one of the top three batting averages in the league that year, but unfortunately the team as a whole didn't do very well and finished eighth. Many players suffered injuries, including Walker himself, and the team started to struggle financially. In 1884, the same year Walker had made his major league debut, he was let go from the team. He hadn't yet recovered from a rib injury, and the team couldn't afford to keep on injured players. Walker continued to play baseball until 1889. He was the last African American payer Minor League Baseball's International League until Jackie Robinson joined the

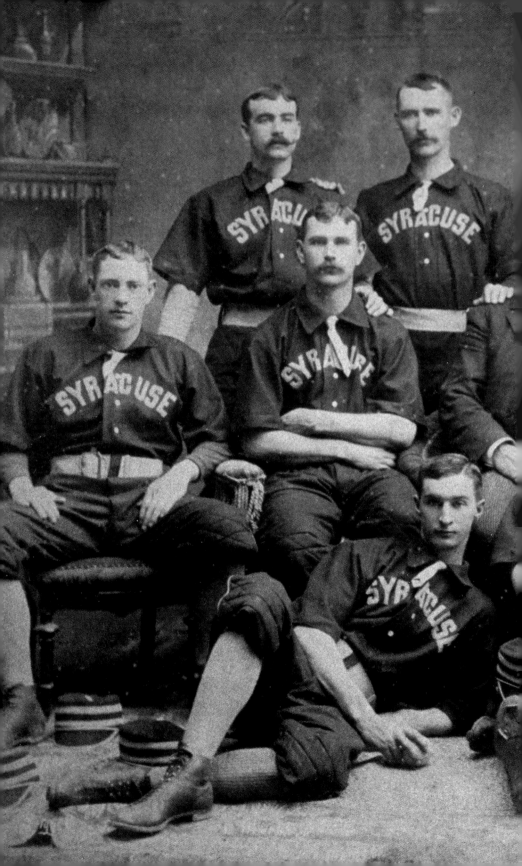

After being let go from the Toledo Blue Stockings, Walker, pictured here on the far right in the back row, played for semiprofessional integrated teams like the Syracuse Stars.

Montreal Royals in 1946 on his way to playing with the Brooklyn Dodgers.

Racism and Discrimination

Like Walker, Bell and his teammates were often subjected to racist remarks. There were many hotels that they could not stay in and restaurants they could not eat in because of racism. Road life was tough, on the field and off.

Entire teams would sometimes travel 100 miles or more in one car to get to a game, and then 100 miles back—all in the same day. In some towns, especially in the South, they would be denied food and drink in restaurants once they got to the town they were scheduled to play in.

When Bell played for the Pittsburgh Crawfords, he and the team would often travel all night in their bus to make it to the next game. The summer heat and long hours were tough on the team, but they still managed to win most of their games. Bell said that they had to learn how to sleep "lying down, sitting, or standing up."

When they were able to stop for rest, they often encountered discrimination. Once, the Crawfords were barred from using the showers in the clubhouse of a stadium they played at in Ohio. Rumor has it that they convinced a woman who owned a rooming house to fill a bathtub with water so they could clean up. Nine players cleaned themselves in the same tub. Getting food was a struggle as well. There was one night when Crawfords players could not find a single restaurant between Akron and Youngstown, Ohio, that would cook for them. Even when they had money, it was hard to find service.

During the Jim Crow era, black Americans were forced to use separate facilities from white Americans, including in bus station waiting rooms.

The players would have to pack food along with their gloves, uniforms, bats, and hats. But this didn't always solve the problem. The players who prepared food for themselves often had it stolen by the players who didn't. One pitcher for the Crawfords, Harry Kincannon, is said to have guarded his food with a pistol. "Anybody eatin' my food tonight is gonna get it with this," he warned his teammates. Once, after Kincannon fell asleep, one of the Crawfords picked up the pistol and removed the bullets. The Crawfords then ransacked Kincannon's bag and passed his food around. After they were done, they draped the left-overs all over him. Kincannon was obviously angry, but he laughed about it with the team when he woke up.

Playing in Latin America

As a result of discriminatory practices in the United States, many African American players preferred to play winter ball in Latin America during the off-season. They were treated better, earned more money, and were shown respect there.

In 1937, while at spring training for the Pittsburgh Crawfords in New Orleans, Bell's teammate Satchel Paige went to play for President Rafael L. Trujillo's baseball team in the Dominican Republic. Trujillo was preparing for an upcoming election. His opponent had imported a ball club that was beating up on almost every club in the Dominican Republic. The nation was in a baseball craze, and at that time a politician's popularity—and chance for reelection—depended heavily on what kind of baseball team he could put in the field. In his bid for reelection, Trujillo sought to build a top-notch team. He wanted Paige and Bell to play for him. This is what Bell said about Satchel's inability to avoid the money offered to him by Trujillo:

> They liked baseball down there. They had a championship series set down there, and they said if Trujillo would win, they would put him back in office: He was pretty near out of office then. So they got guys from Cuba, Panama, and guys out of the Negro Leagues—they had a lot of boys from the States. And they wanted Satchel. He was down in New Orleans training with the Crawfords, and he didn't want to go. So they trailed Satchel to a hotel in New

Orleans. Someone told them Satchel was in there. So two of them went in to look for him, and Satchel slipped out the side door and jumped in his car and tried to get away from them, but they blocked the street and stopped him. These were men from Santo Domingo who were looking for ball players to take down there. Now Satchel was the type of guy that if you showed him money—or a car—you could lead him anywhere. He was that type of fella. He did a lot of wrong things in baseball, but he was easily led. So thcy said they wanted him to go down there, and he said, "I don't wanna go." He had been out in North Dakota already and run off from our team. And we bought a boy from St. Louis named Vincent, and we swapped Vincent out in North Dakota to bring Paige back to the league. So when Vincent went out there and Paige came back to the league, he didn't want to jump again. That's why he was ducking those people. But when they offered him a big salary, then he jumped again and went down there.

In all, nine men from the Pittsburgh Crawfords, including Bell, headed down to the Dominican Republic that year. The best thing about playing *beisbol* in Cuba, Mexico, Puerto Rico, Venezuela, and other Latin American countries was the absence of discrimination and the color line. White and black players were on all the same teams. It also showed how silly the color line was. In Latin American countries, it was obvious that the color of a man's skin had no effect on his ability to play baseball.

Willie Wells of the Newark Eagles had fond memories of playing ball in Mexico. He began spending his summers

Henry Spearman of the Grays runs for the plate as Mule Suttles of the Newark Eagles looks for a ball thrown by Willie Wells on the far right. Like Bell and many other Negro League players, Wells spent time playing in Latin America.

there, too. "Not only do I get more money playing here, but I live like a king. I've found freedom and democracy here, something I never found in the United States. I was branded a Negro in the States and had to act accordingly. Everything I did, including playing ball, was regulated by my color. Well, here in Mexico, I am a man. I can go as far in baseball as I am capable of going."

But playing in Latin America did have its share of hardships. In Santo Domingo, Josh Gibson, Bell, and other Crawfords joined Paige. Trujillo's team had some of the most talented players in baseball's history. But no matter how good they were, they must have feared for their lives. Trujillo told the team that they had to win, or else they would be put to death by a firing squad.

To make sure that the Crawfords knew it was no joke, the players were kept in their hotel and guarded by Trujillo's men when they were not playing. As they played, Trujillo's soldiers were in the stands, carrying rifles with bayonets. The Crawfords played well and won the championship. After winning the championship, they found out that if they had lost, Trujillo's army might have been overthrown, and they might not have ever escaped the country.

Chapter 5

Bell in Retirement

In 1946, after playing for twenty-four years in the Negro Leagues, Bell left the Homestead Grays and retired from playing professionally. He didn't stop playing baseball though. Following his retirement from the Grays, Bell worked as a player-manager for Negro League farm teams, like the Detroit Senators and the Kansas City Stars, for the next four years, helping younger players build skills and get used to playing in a more serious environment. In 1951, he retired fully from playing and became a part-time scout for the St. Louis Browns until 1956, after which he worked as a security officer at St. Louis City Hall.

Bell was known as one of the best Negro League players ever, and he lived up to the name "Cool Papa" for the entirety of his career. Off the field, he was just as calm and kind as he was on it, and he rarely drank or engaged in questionable pursuits. The same couldn't be said for his teammates. Some, like Bell's Crawfords teammate Satchel Paige, messed around simply because they could. Paige knew he was too good to suffer any consequences for things like showing up late to practice or refusing to exercise. Others, like fellow Crawford Josh Gibson, couldn't escape their struggles with addiction. Paige had a long career and a longer life, but Gibson was no so lucky.

The Tragic Death of Josh Gibson

Some said that Gibson drank because he was so frustrated by the unfairness of segregation. It may have been that, or it may have been just the crucl randomness of addiction. In 1943, Gibson was diagnosed with a brain tumor, which was likely related to his drinking and the other drugs he was thought to have used later in life. Gibson passed away in 1947. He was only thirty-six years old.

Cool Papa had fond memories of Gibson's exploits. "One year, Gibson hit 72 home runs that I counted," Bell said. "He would hit more if all the parks had been fenced in like in the majors. Sometimes, the outfielders got back 500 feet and Gibson would still hit the ball over their heads. Have you ever heard of a 500-foot out? But we'd play two, sometimes three games a day, and he would be tired and just couldn't run out those long hits."

During an exhibition game in Yankee Stadium, it is said that Gibson hit a ball out of the stadium not just over the fence, but all the way over the back wall that separates the park from the rest of the Bronx. Bell and others said that they heard about the mammoth shot, but none of them actually saw it. Gibson himself never made the claim, but the story still remains a legend in baseball lore. The story was important to African American ballplayers because it

This statue of Cool Papa Bell is located outside of Busch Stadium in St. Louis, Missouri, and commemorates his contributions to baseball and the city of St. Louis.

meant that Gibson was able to hit the ball farther than Babe Ruth. Gibson was compared to Ruth throughout his career, and the idea that Gibson was getting credit for something Ruth never accomplished helped many African American ballplayers feel that Gibson was finally getting the credit he deserved.

"He was a good catcher, too. Smart," Bell said of Gibson. "He threw a light ball to second. You could catch it bare-handed. Some catchers throw a brick down to second."

Satchel Paige and Josh Gibson played on the same teams for much of their careers, but they did oppose each other while barnstorming. Paige said that Gibson was the best hitter he ever faced, even better than Bell. "You look for his weakness, and while you lookin' for it, he liable to hit forty-five home runs," Paige said.

The biggest difference between Bell, Paige, and Gibson was that the years of struggling to survive in the Negro Leagues burned Gibson out. By 1941, when he was only thirty, Gibson started getting dizzy while chasing after pop-ups. Gibson was a catcher, and it began taking its toll on his knees. He lost a lot of his speed and stopped stealing bases.

By 1942, Gibson was still swatting balls over fences with ease, but it seemed like he was beginning to tire. He complained of painful headaches and turned to alcohol to ease the pain. Gibson had come down with hypertension (high blood pressure), a very serious medical condition. His drinking only made it worse, and the condition had horrible effects on his health and playing ability.

Gibson was still one of the Negro League's premiere hitters in 1943, but in 1944, he hit just six home runs in thirty-nine games. Off the field, he was getting sicker.

He went into depression, was hospitalized for uncontrollable fits of anger, and threatened to commit suicide. Gibson appeared in his last East-West All-Star Game in 1946. He suffered a stroke in January of 1947 while at a movie theater and died the same day. His death shocked Cool Papa Bell and other African American baseball players. It made them wonder if Gibson's unstable mental condition had something to do with the discrimination he endured and the fact that he never made it into the major leagues.

Most Negro League players learned to live with the color line. But Gibson knew that he was one of the greatest sluggers to ever play baseball, and he had been told many times about how much money he could make in the major leagues. In 1942, when major league club owners spent more time scouting Negro League players, Gibson was told by Bill Benswanger, the Pittsburgh Pirates owner, that he was being considered for a major league contract. But the contract never came.

"He was a big, overgrown boy," Jimmie Crutchfield said of Gibson. "He was such a nice guy. But it bothered him that he wasn't going to make the big leagues. It really did. To me it seems that Josh died of a broken heart."

Bell had a photograph of Gibson holding a bat at Griffith Stadium in Washington, D.C. Fans had given him the bat. The words "Josh the Basher" were painted on the bat. "I don't care what league or where it was, Josh hit the long ball more often than any other player I've ever seen. Anyone!" Bell said.

The Kansas City Stars

In 1948, the year after Gibson died, Tom Baird and J.L. Wilkinson, who were co-owners of the Kansas City

Jimmie Crutchfield played with Bell on the Pittsburgh Crawfords. He was an outfielder in the Negro Leagues from 1930 to 1941 before joining the military during World War II.

Monarchs, called on Bell and hired him to manage their minor league team. The contract was written so that Bell's team was called the Kansas City Stars or the Kansas City Travelers when they were playing near Kansas City. When they played outside the midwestern United States, the team was called the Kansas City Monarchs.

Bell managed the team until 1950. In those three seasons, Bell coached Ernie Banks and Elston Howard. Both Howard and Banks went on to become major league stars. Banks said that Bell was responsible for taking him from the Texas sandlots to Kansas City. Both Lou Brock and Maury Wills say that Bell played a part in teaching them the art of base stealing.

It is said that Bell was offered a job to play for the major league St. Louis Browns club in 1948, but he turned it down. By that time, he was already forty-five years old and past his prime.

Baseball did not leave Bell rich. There were no pensions for Negro League ballplayers, so Bell had to continue working. After he ended his playing and coaching career, he worked as a custodian for city hall in St. Louis. He was promoted to night watchman of city hall and ended up working for the city for twenty-one years. He retired in 1973.

Bell's Final Years

Bell spent his remaining thirty-five years in a solid red-brick duplex at 3034 Dickson Street in St. Louis, Missouri. He and his wife, Clara, lived off of the meager income from Social Security checks, a pension from the city of St. Louis, and a stipend from the baseball commissioner's office. In recognition of Bell's contributions to the city of St. Louis

Mr. Sunshine

One of the players Bell coached in Kansas City was Ernie Banks, a shortstop and first baseman who would go on to play for the Chicago Cubs for eighteen years. It's said that Cool Papa Bell saw Banks playing softball with his church team and invited him to start playing with the Kansas City Monarchs, launching Banks's baseball career. Banks joined the Cubs in 1953, six years after Jackie Robinson first broke the Major League Baseball color line, and he was the Cubs' first black player. He was known on the Cubs as "Mr. Cub" and "Mr. Sunshine" for his always positive attitude. At bat, Banks was a slugger, and he was the leading home run hitter in the National League for two seasons. Banks was inducted into the Hall of Fame in 1977, three years after the induction of Bell, the man who made him a baseball player.

and the game of baseball, Dickson Street was renamed James Cool Papa Bell Avenue in the 1980s.

Bell said much of his inspiration to excel in baseball came from his wife, Clara. He married Clara Belle Thompson in 1928 in East St. Louis, Missouri. They were married for sixty-two years when Clara died on January 20, 1991.

Already afflicted with glaucoma, Bell suffered a heart attack on February 27, 1991. He was hospitalized at St. Louis University Hospital and died a week later on March 7, 1991. He was eighty-eight years old.

In Satchel Paige's book, *Maybe I'll Pitch Forever*, Paige summed up Bell's incredible career: "If Cool Papa had known about colleges or if colleges had known about Cool Papa, Jesse Owens would have looked like he was walking."

Bell is buried at St. Peter's Cemetery in St. Louis. He never showed any bitterness or hostility about not being able to play in the major leagues. "Funny, but I don't have any regrets about not playing in the majors. At that time the doors were not open only in baseball, but in other avenues that we couldn't enter. They say that I was born too soon. I say the doors were opened up too late." In his will, he wrote that he wanted to have twelve pallbearers: six black and six white.

"Because of baseball, I smelled the rose of life," Bell said. "I wanted to meet interesting people, to travel, and to have nice clothes. Baseball allowed me to do all those things, and most important, during my time with the Crawfords, it allowed me to become a member of a brotherhood of friendship which will last forever."

Cool Papa Bell was elected to the National Baseball Hall of Fame in Cooperstown, New York, on August 12,

Bell presents St. Louis Cardinal player Lou Brock with a base after Brock broke the MLB record for most bases stolen during a game in 1977.

1974. He was the fifth Negro League star to be inducted at Cooperstown. His St. Louis Stars' uniform and a plaque that describes his career are showcased there today.

Other Negro Leaguers in the Hall of Fame

There have been thirty-one players who spent most of their careers in the Negro Leagues inducted into the Hall of Fame. The very first to be inducted, in 1971, was Satchel Paige, the famous pitcher, for his career of over forty years and success in a number of different leagues. In 1972, Bell's Crawfords teammate Josh Gibson was inducted, along with famed hitter Buck Leonard.

Walter F. "Buck" Leonard was born in September 1907. In his prime, he was one of the Negro Leagues' most feared sluggers. Between 1937 and 1946, he and home-run legend Josh Gibson were the most dangerous 3-4 combination in the Negro Leagues. Leonard was a five-foot-eleven-inch, 185-pound lefty slugger. He had a graceful swing that brought him many long, long hits. He played first base for the Homestead Grays, one of the greatest teams in Negro League history. After leaving baseball, Buck went to work for the city of Rocky Mount, North Carolina, as an assistant probation officer. He died in 1997.

The fourth to be elected was Monte Irvin, in 1973. Monte Irvin, like many great African American athletes of his time, played most of his career in the Negro Leagues. He did make it to the major leagues—with Bell's help—and he played an important role during his eight seasons with the New York Giants. The Giants won two pennants with Irvin. Irvin started his professional baseball career in the Negro Leagues at the age of seventeen. He developed

Clockwise from top left, Mickey Mantle, Whitey Ford, Joco Conlan, and Cool Papa Bell pose with their Hall of Fame plaques after being inducted in 1974.

into a power-hitting, smooth-fielding, base-stealing triple threat. In 1951, Irvin stole home in the World Series. He was inducted into the Hall of Fame in 1973.

In 1974, Bell himself was elected to the Hall of Fame, and in 1975, it was third baseman Judy Johnson's turn. Johnson was a fixture at third base for the Negro National League's Hilldale Club in the 1920s and 1930s. His contemporaries felt he was one of the smartest and slickest fielders in the game. In the first Negro World Series in 1924, he led Hilldale's hitting attack with a .341 batting average. After retiring, he became a major league baseball scout.

Oscar Charleston, the very Charleston who was at bat when Cool Papa got his nickname, was inducted in 1976. He was a mighty hitter over his forty-year career. Between 1915 and 1954, Charleston played for the Indianapolis ABCs, Harrisburg Giants, Homestead Grays, the Pittsburgh Crawfords, Philadelphia Stars, and Indianapolis Clowns. Charleston played first base and center field, and also managed teams. He had running speed, power at the plate, and a powerful throwing arm. Charleston is said to have hit over .400 five times in his career. His lifetime average is .357. Jimmie Crutchfield, who played under Charleston on the Pittsburgh Crawfords, said, "If I had to pick the best player I saw in my time, it would be hard to pick between Charleston and Josh Gibson. When the chips were down and you needed somebody to bat in the clutch— even at his age Charleston was as good as anybody playing baseball."

Martín Dihigo and Pop Lloyd were both inducted in 1977. Martín Dihigo was a stellar performer at whatever position he played—pitching, infield, or outfield. Buck

Leonard called Dihigo the best ballplayer of all time. Dihigo first played professional ball in America in 1923, when he was just fifteen years old. He often started games in center field and later came on to pitch in relief. In 1929, he was credited with hitting .386 in the American Negro League. Along with Cool Papa Bell, Satchel Paige, Josh Gibson, and others, he played several seasons in Latin America in the 1930s and 1940s.

John Henry "Pop" Lloyd played shortstop for at least five different professional Negro League teams: the Philadelphia Giants, the New York Lincoln Giants, the Chicago American Giants, the Brooklyn Royal Giants, and the Atlantic City Bacharach Giants. Most of his contemporaries say that he was the greatest shortstop ever. Even Honus Wagner, his white rival at shortstop, admitted this. Lloyd's career batting average is .339.

Andrew "Rube" Foster, inducted to the hall in 1981, is said to have been the best pitcher of his time, black or white. Rube played twenty-four years for the Chicago American Giants, between 1902 and 1926. He is credited with starting the Negro National League, the strongest of all the Negro Leagues. Foster was a huge man. He weighed about 300 pounds. He was one of the greatest managers ever. As a pitcher, Rube once went 54 and 1 in a season. As a manager, he once led his team to a 126 and 6 record. He is also credited with inventing little ball, the art that Bell perfected and that African American baseball players brought back to the major leagues when Jackie Robinson began playing for the Brooklyn Dodgers in 1947.

Over the next twenty years, from 1985 to 2005, eight more Negro Leaguers were elected to the Hall of Fame.

Thirteen more players were inducted in 2006 alongside executives like Effa Manley and Alex Pompez when the Hall of Fame had a special election held by the Committee on African-American Baseball to vote on Negro Leagues and pre-Negro Leagues candidates. Just a few months after this special election, a new exhibit about the history of African American baseball opened in the Hall of Fame's museum. A full list of Negro League players in the Hall of Fame can be found in the back of this book.

Negro Leaguers in the Hall of Fame

NAME	POSITION	PRIMARY TEAM	DATE INDUCTED
Satchel Paige	Pitcher	Kansas City Monarchs	1971
Josh Gibson	Catcher	Homestead Grays	1972
Buck Leonard	First Baseman	Homestead Grays	1972
Monte Irvin	Left Fielder	Newark Eagles	1973
Cool Papa Bell	Center Fielder	St. Louis Stars	1974
Judy Johnson	Third Baseman	Hilldale Daisies	1975
Oscar Charleston	Center Fielder	Pittsburgh Crawfords	1976
Martín Dihigo	Pitcher	Cuban Stars	1977
Pop Lloyd	Shortstop	New York Lincoln Giants	1977
Rube Foster	Pitcher/Manager	Chicago American Giants	1981
Ray Dandridge	Third Baseman	Newark Eagles	1987
Leon Day	Pitcher	Newark Eagles	1995
Bill Foster	Pitcher	Chicago American Giants	1996
Willie Wells	Shortstop	St. Louis Stars	1997

NAME	POSITION	PRIMARY TEAM	DATE INDUCTED
Bullet Rogan	Pitcher	Kansas City Monarchs	1998
Joe Williams	Pitcher	New York Lincoln Giants	1999
Turkey Stearnes	Center Fielder	Detroit Stars	2000
Hilton Smith	Pitcher	Kansas City Monarchs	2001
Frank Grant	Second Baseman	Cuban Giants	2006
Pete Hill	Center Fielder	Chicago American Giants	2006
José Méndez	Pitcher	Cuban Stars	2006
Louis Santop	Catcher	Hilldale Daisies	2006
Ben Taylor	First Baseman	Indianapolis ABCs	2006
Sol White	Second Baseman/ Executive	Philadelphia Giants	2006
Ray Brown	Pitcher	Homestead Grays	2006
Willard Brown	Outfielder	Kansas City Monarchs	2006
Andy Cooper	Pitcher	Kansas City Monarchs	2006
Biz Mackey	Catcher	Hilldale Giants	2006
Mule Suttles	First Baseman	Newark Eagles	2006
Cristóbal Torriente	Center Fielder	Chicago American Giants	2006
Jud Wilson	Third Baseman	Philadelphia Stars	2006

Timeline

1903

May 17: James Thomas Bell is born near Starkville, Mississippi.

1920

The first viable Negro National League, with eight teams, is established by Rube Foster.

Bell leaves Mississippi and settles in St. Louis, Missouri, where he signs on with the Compton Hill Cubs.

Bell marries Clara Thompson.

1921

The Compton Hill Cubs break up.

1922

Bell pitches for the East St. Louis Cubs, a semiprofessional team.

Bell completes his first full season as a pitcher for the Negro National League's St. Louis Stars, batting over .400.

1924

Bell begins working on his fielding skills and makes a permanent move from pitcher to center field.

1928

Bell and his teammates take the Stars to their first league title.

1932

Bell moves to the Detroit Wolves after the breakup of the Negro National League.

1933

Bell begins a four-year stint with the Pittsburgh Crawfords.

Bell claims to have stolen 175 bases in 200 games during the 1933 season.

Bell is elected to play in his first East-West All-Star Game.

1937

Bell travels to the Dominican Republic and plays for the baseball team of dictator Rafael Trujillo.

1938

Bell travels to Latin America to play in the Mexico League for four years.

1942

Bell returns to the United States to play for the Chicago American Giants of the Negro American League.

1943

Bell moves to the Homestead Grays.

1946

Bell retires from professional baseball.

1947

Jackie Robinson breaks the baseball color line by playing for the Brooklyn Dodgers.

Bell's friend and teammate Josh Gibson passes away.

1948

Bell manages the Kansas City Monarchs.

Timeline

1950

Bell works part-time as a scout for the St. Louis Browns, which later became the Baltimore Orioles.

1951

Bell retires from baseball and takes a job as a custodian and night watchman for city hall in St. Louis.

1973

Bell retires and continues living in St. Louis.

1974

Bell is inducted into the Baseball Hall of Fame.

1991

Bell's wife, Clara, dies in January. Bell suffers a heart attack and dies in March at the age of eighty-eight.

Glossary

barnstorming The act of traveling from town to town to play baseball against local and other traveling teams.

batting average A measure of a batter's performance taken by dividing the total number of hits by the number of times at bat, not including walks.

blackface A racist performance popular in the nineteenth and early twentieth century where a non-black person paints their face in a mockery of a black person.

bunt A ball that is hit very softly. When bunting, hitters do not swing. They hold the bat parallel to the ground in an attempt to bounce the ball a few feet in front of home plate.

clubhouse A room at a ballpark where players can change into their uniforms and prepare for games.

curveball A medium-speed pitch that drops several inches just as it approaches home plate. It is thrown with a different motion than the fastball.

discrimination The unfair treatment of an individual or group based on characteristics like race or gender.

double A base hit that allows the hitter to reach second base safely.

exhibition game A game that has little to no impact on a team's or individual player's statistics or ranking.

farm team A team meant to provide young players with coaching and experience before they move up to a more serious level of play.

fastball The most common pitch, normally thrown between 85 and 95 miles per hour.

franchise A professional sports team.

induct To place a person in a special, honored group or association in recognition of that person's achievements, skill, or talent.

integration To bring parts together. Specifically in the context of baseball, to have African American and white players on the same teams.

juiced ball A tightly wound baseball that travels farther and faster than a normal baseball after it is hit.

knuckleball A pitch that is gripped with a pitcher's knuckles and thrown softly toward the plate without any rotation. Knuckleballs tend to dart up, down, left, or right as they approach the plate.

lead-off The first hitter to bat in an inning.

league A group of teams that play games mostly against other teams in the group.

little ball A baseball strategy in which walks, stolen bases, bunting, and sacrifice hits are very important.

pennant The division or league championship.

rookie A first-year baseball player.

rooming house A private house whose owner rents out rooms for people to stay.

sacrifice bunt A batter who gives up his at-bat by hitting the ball so runners can move over to second or third base. Sacrifices are used when there are less than two outs to increase a team's chances of scoring a run.

segregated Separated, especially based on race.

sharecropper A person who farms someone else's land and gives them part of the crop as rent.

slugger A player who can hit the ball particularly hard and far.

southpaw A left-handed pitcher.

stolen base A base that is taken by a speedy runner. A runner steals by running from one base to the next after a pitch is thrown. The runner must slide safely into the base before the catcher can throw him out in order to steal the base.

switch hitter A batter who bats from both the right and left sides of home plate.

triple A base hit in which the batter reaches third base safely.

white supremacist A person who believes white people are better than anyone else simply because they are white.

Further Reading

Books

Democker, Michael. *Barnstorming.* Kennett Square, PA: Purple Toad Publishing, 2016.

Diprimio, Pete. *Legends of the Leagues.* Kennett Square, PA: Purple Toad Publishing, 2016.

Lester, Larry. *Black Baseball in New York City: An Illustrated History, 1885-1959.* Jefferson, NC: McFarland, 2017.

Panchyk, Richard. *Baseball History for Kids.* Chicago, IL: Chicago Review Press, 2016.

Sturm, James, and Rich Tommaso. *Satchel Paige: Striking Out Jim Crow.* New York, NY: Disney-Hyperion, 2019.

Websites

"Cool Papa Bell," Black History Now
http://blackhistorynow.com/cool-papa-bell
The Black History Now site, from the Black Heritage
Commemorative Society, has an enormous collection
of biographies of famous black Americans, including
Cool Papa Bell and other Negro Leaguers.

Major League Baseball's "Negro Leagues Legacy"
mlb.mlb.com/mlb/history/mlb_negro_leagues.jsp
The official website of Major League Baseball offers a
huge archive of Negro Leagues history and images.

National Baseball Hall of Fame
baseballhall.org/hall-of-famers
The Baseball Hall of Fame's official website has lots of
historical articles and information about individual Hall
of Famers to explore.

Negro Leagues Baseball Museum
www.nlbm.com/s/index.cfm
The Negro Leagues Baseball Museum was founded in
1990 and is located in Kansas City, Missouri.

Index

About the Author

Hallie Murray is an editor who lives and works in New York. Originally from New Jersey, she studied English literature at Bowdoin College and Oxford University before beginning her career in publishing at an academic press. Outside of work, she enjoys ultimate Frisbee and long-distance running. She also loves cooking, music, and the *New York Times* crossword.